# STRONG FAITH

# STRONG FAITH

# C.H. Spurgeon

Whitaker House

**STRONG FAITH**

ISBN: 0-88368-341-5
Printed in the United States of America
Copyright © 1995 by Whitaker House
Images © 1995 PhotoDisc, Inc.

Whitaker House
580 Pittsburgh Street
Springdale, PA 15144

2 3 4 5 6 7 8 9 10 / 04 03 02 01 00 99 98 97 96

# *Contents*

# Contents

# *Introduction*

*He that believeth on Him is
not condemned.
—John 3:18*

The way of salvation is stated in
Scripture in the very plainest
terms, and yet, perhaps, there is no
truth about which more errors have
been uttered than concerning the faith
which saves the soul. Well has it been
proved by experience that all doctrines
of Christ are mysterious—mysterious,
not so much in themselves, but because they are *"hid to them that are
lost, in whom the god of this world
hath blinded the minds of them that
believe not"* (2 Corinthians 4:3-4). So
plain is Scripture, that one would have
said, "He who runs may read." However, so dim is man's eye and so

7

marred is his understanding, that the very simplest truth of Scripture he distorts and misrepresents.

Indeed, beloved, even those who know what faith is, personally and experientially, do not always find it easy to give a good definition of it. They think they have hit the mark, and then, afterwards, they lament that they have failed. Straining themselves to describe some one part of faith, they find they have forgotten another. In the excess of their earnestness to clear the poor sinner out of one mistake, they often lead him into a worse error. Thus, I think I may say that, while faith is the simplest thing in all the world, yet it is one of the most difficult about which to write. Because of its very importance, the soul begins to tremble while speaking of it, and then we are not able to describe it as clearly as we would like.

I intend, by God's help, to put together various thoughts on faith, each of which I may have spoken at different times, but which have not been collected before, and which, I have no doubt, have been misunderstood from the lack of their having been put together in their proper order. I will address these points:

1. The object of faith—to what it looks.
2. The reason of faith—why does any man believe, and from where does his faith come?
3. The ground of the sinner's faith—on what ground he dares to believe on the Lord Jesus Christ.
4. The warranty of faith—why it dares to trust in Christ.
5. The result of faith—how it speeds when it comes to Christ.
6. The satisfactory declaration made in Scripture concerning those who have faith.
7. Misapprehensions about faith, by reason of which Christians are often cast down.
8. What this faith includes.
9. What this faith excludes.

Charles Spurgeon

# Chapter 1

# *The Object of Faith*

*For ye are all the children of God by
faith in Christ Jesus.*
*—Galatians 3:26*

I am told in the Word of God to
believe—what am I to believe? I am
bidden to look—to what am I to look?
What is to be the object of my hope,
belief, and confidence? The reply is
simple: **The object of faith for a
sinner is Christ Jesus**. How many
make a mistake about this and think
that they are to believe on God the Father! Belief in God is an after-result of
faith in Jesus. We come to believe in
the eternal love of God the Father as

the result of trusting the precious blood of the Son.

Many men say, "I would believe in Christ if I knew that I were elect." This is coming to the Father, and no man can come to the Father except by Christ (see John 14:6). It is the Father's work to elect. You cannot come directly to Him: therefore you cannot know your election until first you have believed on Christ the Redeemer. Then through redemption, you can approach the Father and know your election.

Some, too, make the mistake of looking to the work of God the Holy Spirit. They look within to see if they have certain feelings. If they find them, their faith is strong; but if their feelings have departed from them, then their faith is weak. Thus, they look to the work of the Spirit, which is not the object of a sinner's faith.

Both the Father and the Spirit must be trusted in order to complete redemption, but for the particular mercy of justification and pardon the blood of the Mediator is the only plea.

Christians have to trust the Spirit after conversion. However, the sinner's business, if he would be saved, is not with trusting the Spirit nor with looking to the Spirit, but looking to Christ Jesus, and to Him alone. I know your salvation depends on the whole Trinity, but yet the first and immediate object of a sinner's justifying faith is neither God the Father, nor God the Holy Ghost, but God the Son, incarnate in human flesh, and offering atonement for sinners.

Do you have the eye of faith? Then, soul, look to Christ as God. If you would be saved, believe Him to be God over all, blessed forever. Bow before Him, and accept Him as being "very God of very God." If you do not, you have no part in Him.

When you have thus believed, then believe in Him as man. Believe the wondrous story of His incarnation. Rely on the testimony of the evangelists who declare that the Infinite was robed in the infant, that the Eternal was concealed within the mortal, that

He who was King of heaven became a servant of servants and the Son of man. Believe and admire the mystery of His incarnation, for unless you believe this, you cannot be saved.

Then especially, if you would be saved, let your faith behold Christ in his perfect righteousness. See Him keeping the law without blemish, obeying His Father without error, preserving His integrity without flaw. All this you are to consider as being done on your behalf. You could not keep the law; He kept it for you. You could not obey God perfectly; His obedience stands in the stead of your obedience— by it you are saved.

But take care that your faith clearly fixes itself upon Christ as dying and as dead. View the Lamb of God as dumb before His shearers. See Him as the *"man of sorrows and acquainted with grief"* (Isaiah 53:3). Go with Him to Gethsemane and behold Him sweating drops of blood.

Mark that your faith has nothing to do with anything within yourself. The object of your faith is nothing within you, but something without you. Believe on Him, then, who, on that tree with nailed hands and feet, poured out His life for sinners. There is the object of your faith for justification: not in yourself, nor in anything which the Holy Spirit has done in you, or anything He has promised to do for you. You are to look to Christ and to Christ alone.

Then let your faith behold Christ as rising from the dead. See Him—He has borne the curse, and now He receives the justification. He dies to pay the debt. He rises that He may nail the handwriting of that discharged debt to the cross. See Him ascending up on high, and behold Him this day pleading before the Father's throne. He is there pleading for His people, offering up today His authoritative petition for all that come to God by Him. And He—as God, as man, as living, as dying, as rising, and as reigning above—He, and He alone, is to be the object of your faith for the pardon of sin.

In nothing else must you trust. Christ is to be the only prop and pillar of your confidence. All else you add thereunto will be a wicked antichrist, a rebellion against the sovereignty of the Lord Jesus. But take care if your faith is to save you, that while you look to Christ in all these matters, you view Him as being your substitute.

This doctrine of substitution is so essential to the whole plan of salvation that I must explain it here for the thousandth time. God is just—He must punish sin. God is merciful—He wills to pardon those who believe in Jesus. How is this to be done? How can He be just and exact the penalty, but still be merciful and accept the sinner? He does it so: He takes the sins of His people and actually lifts them from off His people onto Christ. They can then stand innocent as though they had never sinned, and Christ is looked on by God as though He had been all the sinners in the world rolled into one. The sins of His people were taken from their persons, really and actually—not typically and metaphorically—and truly laid on Christ. Then God came forth with His fiery sword to meet the sinner and to punish him. He met Christ. Christ was not a sinner Himself, but the sins of His people were all imputed to Him. Justice, therefore, met Christ as though He had been the sinner, punished Christ for His people's sins, punished Him as far as its rights could go, exacted from Him the last atom of the penalty, and left not a dreg in the cup.

Now, the person who can see Christ as being his substitute, and puts his trust in Him, is thereby delivered from the curse of the law. Soul, when you see Christ obeying the law, your faith is to say, "He obeys that for His people." When you see Him dying, you are to count the burgundy drops and say, "Thus He took my sins away." When you see Him rising from the dead, you are to say, "He rises as the head and representative of all His elect." And when you see Him sitting at the right hand of God, you are to view Him there as the pledge that all for whom He died will most surely sit at the Father's right hand.

Learn to look on Christ as being in God's sight as though He were the sinner. *"In him is no sin"* (1 John 5:3). *"For Christ also hath once suffered for sins, the just for the unjust"* (1 Peter 3:18). He was the righteous, but He stood in the place of the unrighteous. All that the unrighteous ought to have endured, Christ has endured once for all, and put away their sins forever by the sacrifice of Himself.

This is the great object of faith. I pray you, do not make any mistake about this, for a mistake here will be dangerous, if not fatal. By your faith, see Christ, in His life, death, sufferings, and resurrection, as being the substitute for all whom His Father gave Him—the vicarious sacrifice for the sins of all those who will trust Him with their souls. Christ, then, thus set forth, is the object of justifying faith.

Now, let me further remark that there are some who may read this, no doubt, who will say, "Oh, I would believe and I would be saved if..." If what? If Christ had died? "Oh no, sir, my doubt is nothing about Christ." I thought so. Then what is the doubt? "Why, I would believe if I felt this, or if I had done that." So you think you would. But I tell you that you would not believe in Jesus if you felt that way or if you had done whatever, for then you would believe in yourself and not in Christ. That is the plain truth of it. If you were So-and-So, then you could have confidence. Confidence in what? Why, confidence in your feelings and confidence in your actions, which is clearly contrary to confidence in Christ.

Faith is not to infer from something good within me that I will be saved. Rather, it is to say determinedly and despite all feelings, "I am guilty in the sight of God and deserve His wrath. Yet I do nevertheless believe that *'the blood of Jesus Christ his Son cleanseth me from all sin"* (1 John 1:7). Though my present consciousness condemns me, yet my faith overpowers my consciousness, and I do believe, *'he is able to save to the uttermost them that come unto God by him'* (Hebrews 7:25)."

To come to Christ as a saint is very easy work. To trust to a doctor to cure you when you believe you are getting better is very easy. But to trust your physician when you feel as if the sentence of death were in your body, to bear up when the disease is rising in your very skin and when the ulcer is gathering its venom, to believe even then in the efficacy of the medicine— that is faith.

And so, when sin gets the master of you, when you feel that the law condemns you, then, even then, as a sinner, to trust Christ, this is the most daring feat in all the world. The faith which shook down the walls of Jericho, the faith which raised the dead, the faith which stopped the mouths of lions, was not greater than that of a poor sinner who dares to trust the blood and righteousness of Jesus

Christ when he is in the jaws of all his sins. Do this, soul, then you are saved, whoever you may be.

The object of saving faith, then, is Christ as the substitute for sinners. God in Christ, but not God apart from Christ, nor any work of the Spirit, but the work of Jesus only must be viewed by you as the foundation of your hope.

# Chapter 2

# *The Reason of Faith*

*Faith cometh by hearing.*
*—Romans 10:17*

Granted, but of all men who hear, do not many still remain unbelieving? How, then, does any man come by his faith? To his own experience, his faith comes as the result of a sense of need. The man feels himself needing a Savior. He finds Christ to be just such a Savior as he wants. Therefore, because he cannot help himself, he believes in Jesus. Having nothing of his own, he feels he must take Christ or else perish. Thus, he does it because he cannot help doing it. He is boxed into a corner, and there is but this one way of escape, namely, by the righteousness of another. He feels he cannot escape by any good deeds or sufferings of his own. Thus, he comes to Christ and humbles himself, because he cannot do without Christ and must perish unless he lays hold of Him.

But to carry the question further back, where does that man get his sense of need? How is it that he, rather than others, feels his need of Christ? It is certain he has no more necessity for Christ than other men. How does he come to know, then, that he is lost and ruined? How is it that he is driven by the sense of ruin to take hold of Christ, the Restorer?

The reply is, this is the gift of God; this is the work of the Spirit. *"No man can come to* [Christ] *except the Father...draw him"* (John 6:44), and the Father through the Spirit draws men to Christ by shutting them up under the law to a conviction that if they do not come to Christ they must perish. Then by sheer stress of weather, they tack about and run into this heavenly port. Salvation by Christ is so disagreeable to our carnal mind, so inconsistent with our love of human merit, that we never would take Christ to be our all in all, if the Spirit did not convince us that we were nothing and did not so compel us to lay hold of Christ.

But, then, the question goes even further back. How is it that the Spirit of God teaches some men their need, and not other men? Why is it some of you were driven by your sense of need to Christ, while others go on in their self-righteousness and perish? There is no answer to be given but this, *"Even so, Father, for so it seemed good in thy sight"* (Matthew 11:26). In the end, it comes down to divine sovereignty. The Lord has *"hid these things from the wise and prudent, and hath revealed them unto babes"* (Luke 10:21).

The way in which Christ put it was: *"My sheep hear my voice...ye believe not because ye are not of my sheep, as I said unto you"* (John 10:27, 26). Some divines would like this to read, "You are not my sheep, because you do not believe," as if believing made us the sheep of Christ. But it says, *"Ye believe not because ye are not of my sheep."*

*"All that the Father giveth me shall come to me."* (John 6:37). If they come not, it is a clear proof that they were never given. Those who were given of old eternity to Christ, chosen of God the Father, and then redeemed by God the Son—these are led by the Spirit, through a sense of need, to come and lay hold of Christ.

No man ever did, or ever will, believe in Christ unless he feels his need of Him. No man ever did, or will, feel his need of Christ unless the Spirit makes him feel, and the Spirit will make no man feel his need of Jesus savingly, unless it is written in that eternal book, in which God has surely engraved the names of His chosen.

So, then, I hope I am not to be misunderstood on this point: The reason of faith, or why men believe, is God's electing love working through the Spirit by a sense of need, to bring them to Christ Jesus.

# Chapter 3

# *The Ground of the Sinner's Faith*

**M**y dear friends, I have already said that no man will believe in Jesus, unless he feels his need of him. I have often said, and I repeat it again, that I do not come to Christ pleading that I feel my need of Him. My reason for believing in Christ is not that I feel my need of Him, but that I have a need of Him.

The ground on which a man comes to Jesus is not as a sensible sinner, but as a sinner, and nothing but a sinner. He will not come unless he is awakened. But when he comes, he does not say, "Lord, I come to you because I am an awakened sinner. Save me." Rather he says, "Lord, I am a sinner. Save me." Not his awakening, but his sinnership is the method and plan upon which he dares to come.

You will, perhaps, perceive what I mean, for I cannot exactly explain myself just now. In reference to the preaching of a great many Calvinistic divines, they will say to a sinner, "Now, if you feel your need of Christ, if you have repented so much, if you have been scoured by the law to such and such a degree, then you may come to Christ on the ground that you are an awakened sinner." I say that is false. No one may come to Christ on the ground of his being an awakened sinner. A person must come to him as a sinner.

When I come to Jesus, I know I cannot come unless I am awakened, but, nevertheless, I do not come as an awakened sinner. I do not stand at the foot of His cross to be washed because I have repented. I bring nothing when I come but sin. A sense of need is a good feeling, but when I stand at the foot of the cross, I do not believe in Christ because I have got good feelings, but I believe in Him whether I have good feelings or not.

> Just as I am without one plea,
> But that thy blood was shed for me,
> And that thou bidst me come to thee,
> O Lamb of God, I come.

Mr. Roger, Mr. Sheppard, Mr. Flavell, and several excellent divines in the Puritanic age, and especially Richard Baxter, used to give descriptions of what a man must feel before he would dare to come to Christ. Now, I say in the language of Mr. Fenner, another of those divines, who said he was but a babe in grace when compared to the others:

> I dare to say it, that all this is not scriptural. Sinners do feel these things before they come, but they do not come on the ground of having felt it; they come on the ground of being sinners, and on no other ground whatever.

The gate of mercy is opened, and over the door it is written, "This is a faithful saying and worthy of all acceptation, that Christ Jesus came into the world to save sinners" (1 Timothy 1:15). Between that word *"save"* and the next word *"sinners,"* there is no adjective. It does not say, "penitent sinners," "awakened sinners," "sensible sinners," "grieving sinners," or "alarmed sinners." No, it only says *"sinners."*

I know this, that when I come, I come to Christ today, for I feel it is as much a necessity of my life to come to the cross of Christ today as it was to come ten years ago. When I come to him, I dare not come as a conscious sinner, or an awakened sinner, but I have to come still as a sinner with nothing in my hands. I saw an aged man lately in the vestry of a chapel in Yorkshire. I had preached something to this effect. The old man had been a Christian for years, and he said, "I never saw it put exactly so, but still I know that is just the way I come. I say:

'Nothing in my hands I bring,
Simply to thy cross I cling;
Naked, look to thee for dress;
Helpless, come to thee for grace;
Black—

("Black enough," said the old man.)

'I to the fountain fly,
Wash me, Savior, or I die.'"

Faith is getting out of yourself and getting into Christ. I know that many hundreds of poor souls have been troubled because the minister has said, "if you feel your need, you may come to Christ." "But," say they, "I do not feel my need enough. I am sure I do not."

Many scores of letters have I received from poor troubled consciences who have said, "I would venture to believe in Christ to save me if I had a tender conscience, if I had a soft heart. But oh, my heart is like a rock of ice which will not melt. I cannot feel as I would like to feel, and therefore I must not believe in Jesus." Oh! Away with

this wicked antichrist spirit. It is not
your soft heart that entitles you to believe. You are to believe in Christ to
renew your hard heart, and come to
Him with nothing about you but sin.

The ground on which a sinner
comes to Christ is that he is black:
that he is dead, and not that he knows
he is dead; that he is lost, and not that
he knows he is lost. I know he will not
come unless he does know it, but that
is not the ground on which he comes.
It is the secret reason why, but it is
not the public, positive ground which
he understands. Here was I, year after
year, afraid to come to Christ because I
thought I did not feel enough. I used to
read that hymn of Cowper's about being insensible as steel:

> If aught is felt, 'tis only pain
>   To find I cannot feel.

When I believed in Christ, I
thought I did not feel at all. Now when
I look back, I find that all the time I
had been feeling most acutely and

intensely, and most of all because I thought I did not feel.

Generally, the people who repent the most think they are impenitent. People feel most their need when they think they do not feel at all, for we are no judges of our feelings. Hence the gospel invitation is not put upon the ground of anything of which we can be a judge. It is put on the ground of our being sinners, and nothing but sinners.

Says one, "It says, *'Come unto me all ye that are weary and heavy laden and I will give you rest'* (Matthew 11:28). Then we must be weary and heavy laden." So it is in that text, but another says: *"Whosoever will, let him* [come and] *take of the water of life freely"* (Revelation 22:17). That does not say anything about *"weary and heavy laden."*

Besides, while the invitation is given to the weary and heavy laden, you will perceive that the promise is not made to them as weary and heavy laden, but it is made to them as coming to Christ. They did not know that they

were weary and burdened when they
came. They thought they were not.
They really were, but part of their
weariness was that they could not be
as weary as they would like to be, and
part of their load was that they did not
feel their load enough. They came to
Christ just as they were. He saved
them, not because there was any merit
in their weariness, or any efficacy in
their being loaded down, but He saved
them as sinners and nothing but sinners. So they were washed in His blood
and made clean.

My dear reader, do let me put this
truth home to you: **If you will come
to Christ as nothing but a sinner,
He will not cast you out.** Old Tobias
Crisp says in one of his sermons upon
this very point, "I dare to say it, but if
you do come to Christ, whosoever you
may be, if He does not receive you,
then He is not true to his word, for He
says, *'Him that cometh to me, I will in
no wise cast out'* (John 6:37)."

If you come to Christ, never mind
qualification or preparation. He needs

no qualification of duties or of feelings
either. You are to come just as you are.
If you are the biggest sinner from hell,
you are as fit to come to Christ as if
you were the most moral and excellent
of men. There is a bath: who is fit to
be washed? A man's blackness is no
reason why he should not be washed,
but the clearer reason why he should
be. When our city magistrates gave relief to the poor, nobody said, "I am so
poor that I am not fit to have relief."
Your poverty is your preparation. The
blackness becomes the white here.
What a strange contradiction!

The only thing you can bring to
Christ is your sin and your wickedness.
All He asks is that you will come
empty-handed, except for your sin. If
you have anything of your own, you
must leave all before you come. If
there is anything good in you, you
cannot trust Christ. You must come
with nothing in your hand. Take Him
as all in all. That is the only ground
upon which a poor soul can be saved—
as a sinner, and nothing but a sinner.

# Chapter 4

# *The Warranty of Faith*

Is it not foolhardy for any man to trust Christ to save him, especially when he has no good thing whatever in himself? Is it not an arrogant presumption for any man to trust Christ? No, dear ones, it is not. It is a grand and noble work of God the Holy Spirit for a man to give the lie to all his sins, and still set his heart and mind that God is true, and believe in the virtue of the blood of Jesus.

But why does any man dare to believe in Christ? I will ask you now. "Well," says one man, "I summoned faith to believe in Christ because I felt there was a work of the Spirit in me."

You do not believe in Christ at all. "Well," says another, "I thought that I had a right to believe in Christ, because I felt somewhat." You had not any right to believe in Christ at all on such a surety as feelings.

What is a man's authorization then for believing in Christ? Here it is: Christ tells him to do it—that is his warrant. Christ's word is the license of the sinner for believing in Christ—not what he feels, nor what he is, nor what he is not, but that Christ has told him to do it. The Gospel goes like this: *"Believe on the Lord Jesus Christ and thou shalt be saved"* (Acts 16:31). *"He that believeth not shall be damned"* (Mark 16:16).

Faith in Christ, then, is a commanded duty as well as a blessed privilege. What a mercy it is that it is a duty, because there never can be any question but that a man has a right to do his duty. Now, on the basis that God commands me to believe, I have a right to believe, whoever I may be. The Gospel is sent to every creature (see

Mark 16:15). Well, I belong to that tribe: I am one of the every creatures. That same Gospel commands me to believe, and I do it. I cannot have done wrong in doing it, for I was commanded to do so. I cannot be wrong in obeying a command of God.

It is a command of God given to every creature that he should believe on Jesus Christ, whom God has sent. This is your authorization, sinner, and a blessed warrant it is, for it is one which hell cannot refute and heaven cannot withdraw. You need not search within to look for the misty confirmation in your experience. You need not look to your works or your feelings to get some dull and insufficient surety for your confidence in Christ. You may believe Christ because He tells you to do so. That is sure ground to stand on, and one which admits no doubt.

Suppose that we are all starving; the city has been besieged and shut down; there has been a long, long famine; and we are ready to die of hunger. There comes an invitation to us to journey at once to the palace of some great prince, there to enjoy a great feast. But we have grown foolish and will not accept the invitation. Suppose now that some hideous madness has gotten hold of us, so that we prefer to die and would rather starve than go.

Suppose the king's herald should say, "Come and feast, poor hungry souls. And because I know you are unwilling to come, I add this threat: if you do not come, my warriors will be upon you; they will make you feel the sharpness of their swords." I think, my dear friends, we should say, "We bless the great man for that threat, because now we need not say, 'I may not come,' while the fact is we may not stay away. Now I need not say I am not fit to come, for I am commanded to come, and I am threatened if I do not come. I will even go."

That awful sentence, *"He that believeth not shall be damned"* (Mark 16:16), was added not out of anger, but because the Lord knew our silly madness, and that we would refuse our own mercies unless He thundered at us to make us come to the feast. *"Compel them to come in"* (Luke 14:23) was the word of the Master of old, and that verse is part of the carrying out of the exhortation, *"Compel them to come in."*

Sinner, you cannot be lost by trusting Christ, but you will be lost if you do not trust Him and lost for not trusting Him. Sinner, not only may you come, but, I pray you, do not defy the wrath of God by refusing to come. The gate of mercy stands wide open. Why will you not come? Why will you not? Why be so proud? Why will you still refuse His voice and perish in your sins?

Mark this: If you perish, any one of you, your blood lies not at God's door, nor Christ's door, but at your own. He can say of you, "You would not come unto Me that you might have life." Poor trembler, if you are willing to come, there is nothing in God's Word to keep you from coming, but there are both threats to drive you, and powers to draw you.

Still I hear you say, "I must not trust Christ." You may, I say, for every creature under heaven is commanded to do it, and what you are commanded to do, you may do. "Ah, well," says one, "still I do not feel that I may." There you are again. You say you will not do what God tells you because of some stupid feelings of your own. You are not told to trust Christ because you feel anything, but simply because you are a sinner.

Now, you know you are a sinner. "I am," says one, "and that is my sorrow." Why your sorrow? That is some sign that you do feel. "Ay," someone says, "but I do not feel enough. That is why I sorrow. I do not feel as deeply as I should." Well, suppose you do feel, or suppose you do not, you still are a sinner. *"This is a faithful saying and worthy of all acceptation that Christ Jesus came into the world to save sinners"* (1 Timothy 1:15).

"Oh, but I am such an old sinner. I have been sixty years in sin." Where is it written that after sixty you cannot be saved? Sir, Christ could save you at a hundred years old—ay, if you were a Methuselah in guilt. *"The blood of Jesus Christ his Son cleanseth us from all sin"* (1 John 1:7). *"Whosoever will, let him* [come and] *take the water of life freely"* (Revelation 22:17). *"He is able to save them to the uttermost that come unto God by him"* (Hebrews 7:25). "Yes," says one, "but I have been a drunkard, a swearer, lascivious, profane." Then you are a sinner. You have not gone further than the uttermost, and He is able to save you still.

"Ay," says another, "but you do not know how my guilt has been aggravated." That only proves you to be a sinner, and that you are commanded to trust Christ and be saved. "Ay," cries yet another, "but you do not know how often I have rejected Christ." Yes, but that only makes you all the more a sinner. "You do not know how hard my heart is." Perhaps not, but that only proves that you are a sinner, and still proves you to be one whom Christ came to save.

"Oh, but sir, I have not any good thing. If I had, you know, I should have something to encourage me." The fact of your not having any good thing just proves to me that you are the man I am sent to preach to. Christ came to save that which was lost, and all you have said only proves that you are lost. Therefore, He came to save you. Do trust Him. Do trust Him.

"But if I am saved," says one, "I will be the biggest sinner that ever was saved." Then the greater music in heaven when you get there. The more glory to Christ, for the bigger the sinner, the more honor to Christ when at last he is brought home. "But my sin has abounded." His *"grace did much more abound"* (Romans 5:20). "But my sin has reached even to heaven." Yes, but His mercy reaches above the heavens (see Psalm 108:4). "Oh! But my guilt is as broad as the world." Yes, but his righteousness is broader than a thousand worlds. "Ay, but my sin is scarlet." Yes, but His blood is more scarlet than your sins, and can wash the scarlet out by a richer scarlet. "But I deserve to be lost, and death and hell cry for my damnation." Yes, and so they may, but the blood of Jesus Christ can cry louder than either death or hell; and it cries today, "Father, let the sinner live."

Oh! I wish I could get this thought out of my own mouth and get it into your heads, that when God saves you, it is not because of anything in you, it is because of something in Himself. God's love has no reason except in His own heart. God's reason for pardoning a sinner is found in His own heart, and not in the sinner. There is as much reason in you why you should be saved as why another should be saved, namely, no reason at all. There is no reason in you why He should have mercy on you, but there is no reason necessary, for the reason lies in God and in God alone.

## Chapter 5

# *The Result of Faith*

There is a man here who has just this moment believed. He is not condemned, but he has spent fifty years in sin and has plunged into all manner of vice. "[His] *sins, which are many, are forgiven*" (Luke 7:47). He stands in the sight of God now as innocent as though he had never sinned.

Such is the power of Jesus' blood that *"he that believeth on him is not condemned"* (John 3:18). Does this relate to what is to happen at the day of judgment? I pray, look at God's Word and you will find it does not say, "He that believeth **shall** not be condemned," but rather that it says, *"is*

*not condemned"*—he **is not now**. And
if he is not now, then it follows that he
never shall be: having believed in
Christ, that promise still stands, *"He
that believeth is not condemned."* I
believe today I am not condemned; in
fifty years' time that promise will be
just the same: *"He that believeth is not
condemned."*

Thus, the moment a man puts his
trust in Christ, he is freed from all
condemnation—past, present, and fu-
ture. From that day, he stands in
God's sight as though he were without
*"spot or wrinkle, or any such thing"*
(Ephesians 5:27). "But he sins," you
say. He does, indeed, but his sins are
not laid to his charge. They were laid
to the charge of Christ of old, and God
can never charge the offense on two—
first on Christ, and then on the sinner.

Someone objects, "Yes, but he often
falls into sin." That may be possible.
However, if the Spirit of God is in him,
he sins not as he was accustomed to
do. He sins by reason of infirmity, not
by reason of his love to sin, for now he

hates it. Mark this. You can object or question in any way you will, and I will still answer, "Yes, but though he sins, yet he is no more guilty in the sight of God. All his guilt has been taken from him and put on Christ—positively, literally and actually lifted off from him and put upon Jesus Christ."

Do you see the Jewish host? There is a scapegoat brought out. The high priest confesses the sin of the people over the scapegoat's head. The sin is all gone from the people and laid upon the scapegoat. Away goes the scapegoat into the wilderness. Is there any sin left on the people? If there is, then the scapegoat has not carried it away. Because it cannot be both here and there, it cannot be carried away and left behind, too. "No," say you, "Scripture says the scapegoat carried away the sin; there was none left on the people when the scapegoat had taken away the sin."

And so, when by faith we put our hand upon the head of Christ, does Christ take away our sin, or does He

not? If He does not, then it is of no use
our believing in Him. But if He really
does take away our sin, then our sin
cannot be on Him and on us too. If it is
on Christ, we are free, clear, accepted,
justified. This is the true doctrine of
justification by faith. As soon as a man
believes in Christ Jesus, his sins are
gone from him, and gone away forever.
They are blotted out now.

Consider a man who owed a hundred pounds. Yet if he has a receipt for
it, he is free. The debt is blotted out.
There is an erasure made in the book,
and the debt is gone. Although a man
commits sin, he is no more a debtor to
the law of God, the debt having been
paid even before the debt was in-
curred.

Does not Scripture say that God
has *"cast all their* [his people's] *sins
into the depths of the sea"* (Micah
7:19)? Now, if they are in the depths of
the sea, they cannot be on His people
too. Blessed be His name, in the day
when He casts our sins into the depths
of the sea, He views us as pure in His

sight, and we stand *"accepted in the Beloved"* (Ephesians 1:6). Then he says, *"As far as the east is from the west, so far hath he removed our transgressions from us"* (Psalm 103:12). They cannot be removed and be here still.

Then, if you believe in Christ, you are no more a sinner in the sight of God. You are accepted as though you were perfect—as though you had kept the law—for Christ has kept it, and His righteousness is yours. You have broken it, but your sin is His, and He has been punished for it. Do not mistake yourselves any longer; you are no more what you were. When you believe, you stand in Christ's place, even as Christ of old stood in your stead. The transformation is complete; the exchange is positive and eternal. They who believe in Jesus are as much accepted of God the Father as His Eternal Son is accepted. And those who believe not, let them do what they will, they can try to work out their own righteousness, but they abide under

the law and still will be under the
curse. Now, you that believe in Jesus,
walk up and down the earth in the
glory of this great truth. You are sinners in yourselves, but you are washed
in the blood of Christ.

David says, *"Wash me, and I shall
be whiter than snow"* (Psalm 51:7).
You have seen the snow come down.
How clear! How white! What could be
whiter? Why, the Christian is whiter
than that. You say, "He is black." I
know he is as black as anyone, as black
as hell. But when the blood-drop of
Christ falls on him, he is white,
*"whiter than snow."* The next time you
see the snow-white crystals falling
from heaven, look on them and say,
"Though I must confess in myself that
I am unworthy and unclean, yet, believing in Christ, He has given me His
righteousness so completely, that I am
even whiter than the snow as it de-
scends from the treasury of God."

Oh! May we have faith to lay hold
of this. Oh, for an overpowering faith
that will get the victory over doubts

and fears, and make us enjoy *"the liberty wherewith Christ has made us free"* (Galatians 5:1). You that believe in Christ, go to your beds this night and say, "If I die in my bed, I cannot be condemned." Should you wake the next morning, go into the world and say, "I am not condemned." When the devil howls at you, tell him, "Ah, you may accuse, but I am not condemned." And if sometimes your sins rise—say, "I know you, but you are all gone forever; I am not condemned." And when your turn does come to die, shut your eyes in peace.

> Bold shall you stand
>     In that great day,
> For who aught to
>     Your charge can lay?

Fully absolved by grace, you will be found at last, and all sin's tremendous curse and blame will be taken away, not because of anything you have done. I pray you do all you can for Christ out of gratitude; but even when you have done all, do not rest there. Rest still in the substitution and the sacrifice. Be what Christ was in His Father's sight. When your conscience bothers you, you can tell it that Christ was for you everything that you ought to have been, that He has suffered all your penalty. Now neither mercy nor justice can strike you, since justice has clasped hands with mercy in a firm covenant to save the man whose faith is in the cross of Christ.

## Chapter 6

# *The Satisfactory Declaration*

*There is, therefore, now no
condemnation to them which are in
Christ Jesus.*
—Romans 8:1

You are aware that in our courts of
law, a verdict of "not guilty"
amounts to an acquittal, and the prisoner is immediately discharged. So is it
in the language of the Gospel: a sentence of "not condemned" imputes the
justification of the sinner. It means
that the believer in Christ receives a
**present justification**. Faith does not
produce its fruits by-and-by, but now.

So far as justification is the result of faith, it is given to the soul in the moment it comes to Christ and accepts Him as its all in all.

Are those who now stand before the throne of God justified today? So are we, as truly and as clearly justified as they who walk in white robes and sing praises above. The thief upon the cross was justified the moment that he turned the eye of faith to Jesus, who was just then hanging by his side. The aged Paul, after years of service, was not more justified than was the thief with no service at all.

We are today *"accepted in the Beloved"* (Ephesians 1:6), today absolved from sin, today innocent in the sight of God. Oh, ravishing, soul-transporting thought! Some clusters of this vine we will not be able to gather until we go to heaven, but this is one of the first ripe clusters, and may be plucked and eaten here. This is not as the corn on the land, which we can never eat until we cross the Jordan. Rather, this is part of the manna in the wilderness and part, too, of our daily raiment with which God supplies us in our journeying here.

We are now—even now—pardoned. Even now our sins are put away. Even now we stand in the sight of God as though we had never been guilty; as innocent as Adam when he stood in integrity, before he had eaten of the forbidden fruit; pure as though we had never received the taint of depravity in our veins. *"There is, therefore, now no condemnation to them which are in Christ Jesus"* (Romans 8:1).

There is not a sin in God's Book, even now, against one of His people. There is nothing laid to their charge. There is neither speck, nor spot, nor wrinkle, nor any such thing remaining upon any single believer in the matter of justification in the sight of the Judge of all the earth.

Further, there is not simply present, but **continual**, **justification**. In the moment when you and I believed, it was said of us, "He is not condemned." Many days have passed since

then, many changes we have seen, but
it is true of us today, "He is not condemned."

The Lord alone knows how long our
appointed days will be—how long before we fulfill the hireling's time, and
flee away like a shadow. But this we
know, since every word of God is assured, and because *"the gifts and call-
ing of God are without repentance"*
(Romans 11:29), though we should live
another fifty years, yet would it still be
written here, *"He that believeth on him
is not condemned."* If by some mysterious dealing in providence our lives
should be lengthened to ten times the
usual limit of man, and we should live
for the eight or nine hundred years of
Methuselah, still would it stand the
same: *"He that believeth on him is not
condemned"* (John 3:18). *"I give unto
them* [My sheep] *eternal life, and they
shall never perish, neither shall any
pluck them out of my hand"* (John
10:28). *"The just shall live by faith"*
(Galatians 3:11). *"He that believeth on
him shall not be confounded."* (1 Peter

2:6). All these promises go to show that the justification which Christ gives to our faith is a continual one, which will last as long as we will live.

Remember, it will last in eternity as well as in time. We will not wear any other dress in heaven but that which we wear here. Today the righteous stand clothed in the righteousness of Christ. They will wear the same wedding dress at the great wedding feast. But what if it should wear out? What if that righteousness should lose its virtue in the eternity to come? Oh, beloved! We entertain no fear about that. Heaven and earth will pass away, but His righteousness will never wax old. No moth will chew it; no thief will steal it; no weeping hand of lamentation will rend it in two.

It must be eternal, even as Christ Jesus our righteousness, is. Because He is our righteousness, the self-existent, the everlasting, the immutable Jehovah, of whose years there is no end and whose strength does not fail, therefore our righteousness has no end; and there will never be any termination of its perfection and its beauty. Scripture, I think, very clearly teaches us that he who believes in Christ has received forever a continual justification.

Again, think for a moment: this justification is **complete**. *"He that believeth on him is not condemned;"* that is to say not in any measure or in any degree. I know some think it is possible for us to be in such a state as to be half-condemned and half-accepted. So far as we are sinners, that far we are condemned; and so far as we are righteous, that far we are accepted. Beloved, there is nothing like that in Scripture. It is altogether apart from the doctrine of the Gospel. If it be of works, it is no more of grace; and if it be of grace, it is no more of works (see Romans 11:6). Works and grace cannot mix and mingle any more than fire and water. It is either one or the other; it cannot be both. The two can never be allied. There can be no mixture of the two, no dilution of one with the other.

He who believes is free from all iniquity, guilt, and blame. Though the devil brings an accusation, it is a false one. We are free even from accusation, since it is boldly challenged, *"Who shall lay any thing to the charge of God's elect?"* (Romans 8:33). It does not say "Who shall prove it?" but *"Who shall lay any thing to* [their] *charge?"* They are so completely freed from condemnation that not even a shadow of a spot on their soul is found, not the slightest passing by of iniquity to cast its black shadow on them. They stand before God not only as half-innocent, but as perfectly so; not only as half-washed, but as *"whiter than snow"* (Psalm 51:7). Their sins are not simply erased, they are blotted out (see Psalm 51:1, 9); not simply put out of sight, but cast into the depths of the sea (see Micah 7:19); not merely gone, and gone as far as the east is from the west (see Psalm 103:12), but gone forever, once for all (see Hebrews 10:10, 12).

You know, beloved, that the Jew in his ceremonial purification, never had his conscience free from sin. After one sacrifice, he needed still another, for these offerings could never make those who came there perfect. The next day's sins needed a new lamb, and the next year's iniquity needed a new victim for an atonement. *"But this man, after he had offered one sacrifice for sins forever, sat down at the right hand of God."* (Hebrews 10:12). No more burnt offerings are needed, no more washing, no more blood, no more atonement, no more sacrifice. Hear the dying Savior cry *"It is finished!"* (John 19:30). Your sins have sustained their death-blow, the robe of your righteousness has received its last thread. It is done, complete, perfect. It needs no addition; it can never suffer any diminution.

Oh, Christian, do lay hold of this precious thought. I may not be able to state it except in weak terms, but let not my weakness prevent your apprehending its glory and its preciousness. This thought is enough to make a man leap, though his legs were chained with irons, and to make him sing, though his mouth were gagged. **We are perfectly accepted in Christ, and our justification is not partial**. It does not go to a limited extent, but goes the whole way. Our unrighteousness is covered. From condemnation we are entirely and irrevocably free.

Again, the non-condemnation is **effectual justification**. The royal privilege of justification shall never miscarry. It will be brought home to every believer.

In the reign of King George III, the son of a member of my church lay under sentence of death for forgery. My predecessor, Dr. Rippon, after incredible exertions, obtained a promise that his sentence would be remitted. By a singular occurrence, the present senior deacon—then a young man—learned from the governor of the jail that the reprieve had not been received, and the unhappy prisoner was to have been executed the next morning. Dr. Rippon went hastily to Windsor, obtained an interview with the monarch in his bedchamber, and received from the king's own hand a copy of that reprieve which had been negligently put aside by a thoughtless officer. "I charge you, Doctor," said his majesty, "to make good speed." "Trust me, Sire, for that," responded the Doctor, and he returned to London just in time, for the prisoner was being marched with many others onto the scaffold.

That pardon might have been given, and yet the man might have been executed if it had not been effectually carried out. But blessed be God, our non-condemnation is an effectual thing. It is not a matter of letter, it is a matter of fact. Poor souls, you know that condemnation is a matter of fact. When you and I suffered in our souls, and were brought under the heavy hand of the law, we felt that its curses were no mock thunders like the wrath of the Vatican, but they were real. We felt that the anger of God was indeed a thing to tremble at—a real substantial fact.

Just as real as the condemnation which justice brings is the justification which mercy bestows. You are not only nominally guiltless, but you are really so, if you believe in Christ. You are not only nominally put into the place of the innocent, but you are really put there the moment you believe in Jesus. Not only is it said that your sins are gone, but they are truly gone. Not only does God look on you as though you were accepted, you are accepted. It is a matter of fact to you, as much a matter of fact as that you sinned. You do not doubt that you have sinned—you cannot doubt that. Likewise, do not doubt then that when you believe, your sins are put away. As certain as the black spot fell on you when you sinned, so certainly and so surely was it all washed away when you were bathed in that fountain filled with blood, which was drawn from Immanuel's veins.

Come, my soul, think about this. You are actually and effectually cleared from guilt. You are led out of your prison. You are no more in fetters as a bond-slave. You are delivered now from the bondage of the law. You are freed from sin, and you can walk at large as a free man. Your Savior's blood has procured your full discharge.

Come, my soul, you have a right now to come to your Father's feet. No flames of vengeance are there to scare you now, no fiery sword. Justice cannot smite the innocent. Come, my soul, your disabilities are taken away. You were unable once to see your Father's face, but you can see it now. You could not speak with Him, nor He with you, but now you have bold *"access by faith into this grace wherein we stand"* (Romans 5:2). Once there was a fear of hell upon you; there is no hell for you now. How can there be punishment for the guiltless? He that believes is guiltless, is not condemned, and cannot be punished. No frowns of an avenging God now. If God is viewed as a Judge, how could He frown on the guiltless? How could the Judge frown upon the absolved one?

More than all the privileges you might have enjoyed if you had never sinned belong to you now that you are justified. All the blessings which you could have had if you had kept the law, and more, are yours today because Christ has kept it for you. All the love and the acceptance which a perfectly obedient being could have obtained of God belong to you, because Christ was perfectly obedient on your behalf, and this imputed all His merits to your account that you might be exceedingly rich through Him who for your sake became exceeding poor (see 2 Corinthians 8:9).

Oh, that the Holy Spirit would but enlarge our hearts, that we might drink sweetness out of these thoughts! There is no condemnation. Moreover, there never will be any condemnation. The forgiveness is not partial, but perfect. It is so effectual that it delivers us from all the penalties of the law, gives to us all the privileges of obedience, and puts us actually high above where we should have been had we never sinned. It fixes our standing more securely than it was before we fell. We are not now where Adam was, for Adam might fall and perish. We are, rather, where Adam would have been if we could suppose God had put him into the garden for seven years, and said, "If you are obedient for seven years, your time of probation will be over, and I will reward you."

The children of God in one sense may be said to be in a state of probation; in another sense there is no probation. There is no probation as to whether the child of God will be saved: he is saved already, his sins are washed away, his righteousness is complete. If that righteousness could endure probation for a million years, it would never be defiled. In fact it always stands the same in the sight of God and must do so forever and ever.

## Chapter 7

# *Misapprehensions about Faith*

*He that believeth is not condemned.*
*—John 3:18*

What simpletons we are! Whatever our natural age, how childish we are in spiritual things! What great simpletons we are when we first believe in Christ! We think that our being pardoned involves a great many things which we afterwards find have nothing whatever to do with our pardon. For instance, we think we will never sin again. We fancy that the battle is all fought, that we have come into a safe field with no more war to wage. We believe, in fact, we have won the victory and have only to stand up and wave the palm branch because it is all over. We imagine that God only has to call us up to Himself, and we will enter heaven without having to fight any enemies on earth.

Now, all these are obvious mistakes. Observe that although it is asserted, *"He that believeth is not condemned,"* yet Scripture never says that he who believes will not have his faith exercised. Your faith will be exercised. An untried faith will be no faith at all. God never gave men faith without intending to try it. Faith is received for the purpose of developing endurance.

Just as our Rifle Corps friends put up the target with the intention of shooting at it, so does God give faith with the intention of letting trials and troubles, sin and Satan, aim all their darts at it. When you have faith in Christ it is a great privilege, but remember that it involves a great trial. When you asked for great faith the other night, did you consider that you asked for great troubles too? You cannot have great faith just to lay up and rust.

Mr. Greatheart, in John Bunyan's *Pilgrim's Progress*, was a very strong man, but then what strong work he had to do! He had to go with all those women and children many scores of times up to the celestial city and back again. He had to fight all the giants, drive back all the lions, slay the giant Slaygood, and knock down the Castle of Despair. If you have a great measure of faith, you will have need to use it all. You will never have a single scrap to spare. You will be like the virgins in our Lord's parable: even though you are a wise virgin, you will have to say to others who might borrow from you, "Not so, lest there be not enough for us and for you."

But when your faith is exercised with trials, do not think you are brought into judgment for your sins. Oh no, believer, there is plenty of exercise, but that is not condemnation.

There are many trials, but still we are justified. We may often be buffeted, but we are never accursed. We may often be cast down, but the sword of the Lord never can and never will smite us to the heart.

Moreover, not only may our faith be exercised, but our faith may come to a very low ebb. Still we are not condemned. When your faith gets so small that you cannot see it, even then you are not condemned. If you have ever believed in Jesus, your faith may be like the sea when it goes out a very long way from the shore, leaving a vast track of mud, and some might say the sea was gone or dried up. But you are not condemned when your faith is almost dried up. And I dare to say, when your faith is at the flood-tide, you are not more accepted then than when your faith is at the lowest ebb. Your acceptance does not depend upon the quantity of your faith, it only depends upon its reality.

If you are really resting in Christ, though your faith may be but a spark, and a thousand devils may try to quench that one spark, yet you are not condemned—you stand accepted in Christ. Though your comforts will necessarily decay as your faith declines, yet your acceptance does not decay. Though faith does rise and fall like the thermometer, though faith is like the mercury in the bulb—all weathers change it—yet God's love is not affected by the weather of earth or the changes of time. Until the perfect righteousness of Christ can be a mutable thing—a football to be kicked about by the feet of fiends—your acceptance with God can never change. You are, you must be, perfectly *"accepted in the Beloved"* (Ephesians 1:6).

There is another thing which often tries the child of God. He at times loses the light of his Father's countenance. Now, remember, it is not said, "He that believeth shall not lose the light of God's countenance." That may happen, but he will not be condemned for all that. You may walk not only for days, but for months, in such a state that you have little fellowship with Christ, very little communion with God of a joyous sort. The promises may seem broken to you; the Bible may afford to you but little comfort. When you turn your eye to heaven, you may only have to feel all the more the smarting that is caused by your Father's rod. You may have vexed and grieved His Spirit, and He may have turned away His face from you. Nevertheless, you are not condemned for all that. Mark the testimony, *"He that believeth is not condemned."*

Even when your Father smites you and leaves a wale at every stroke, and brings blood at every blow, there is not a particle of condemnation in any of His lashes. Not in His anger, but in His dear covenant love, He smites you. There is as unmixed and unalloyed affection in every love stroke of chastisement from your Father's hand as there is in the kisses of Jesus Christ's lips. Oh, believe this. It will tend to lift up your heart. It will cheer you when neither sun nor moon appear. It will honor your God, it will show you where your acceptance really lies. When His face is turned away, believe Him still and say, *"'He abideth faithful'* (2 Timothy 2:13) though He hides His face from me."

I will go a little further still. The child of God may be so assaulted by Satan that he may nearly give up to despair, and yet he is not condemned. The devils may beat the great hell-drum in his ear, until he thinks himself to be on the very brink of perdition. He may read the Bible, and think that every threat is against him and that every promise shuts its mouth and will not cheer him. He may at last sink so low into despondency that he is ready to break the harp that has so long been hanging on the willow (see Psalm 137:2). He may say, "The Lord has quite forsaken me. My God will be gracious no more," but it is not true. He may be ready to swear a thousand times that God's mercy is gone forever and that His faithfulness will fail forevermore; but it is not true! A thousand liars swearing to a falsehood could not make it true, and our doubts and fears are all liars. If there were ten thousand of them, and they all professed the same, it is still a falsehood that God ever did forsake His people or that He ever cast from Him an innocent man. You are innocent, remember, when you believe in Jesus.

"But," say you, "I am full of sin." "Ay," I respond, "but that sin has been laid on Christ." "Oh," you reply, "but I sin daily." "Ay," say I, "but that sin was laid on Him before you committed it, years ago. It is not yours. Christ has taken it away once for all. You are a righteous man by faith, and God will not forsake the righteous, nor will He cast away the innocent."

Thus, I say the child of God may have his faith at a low ebb. He may lose the light of his Father's countenance. He may even get into thorough despair. Yet all these cannot disprove God's word, *"He that believeth is not condemned."*

"But what," say you, "if the child of God should sin?" It is a deep and tender subject, yet we must touch it and be bold here. I would not mince God's truth, lest any should make a bad use of it. I know there are some, not the people of God, who will say, "Let us sin, that grace may abound." Their condemnation is just. I cannot abide the perversion of truth. There are always men who will take the best of food as though it were poison and make the best of truth into a lie, thus damning their own souls.

You ask, "What if a child of God should fall into sin?" I answer, the child of God does fall into sin. Every day he mourns and groans because when he would do good, evil is present with him (see Romans 7:21). But though he falls into sins, he is not condemned for all—not by one of them, or by all of them put together—because his acceptance does not depend upon himself, but upon the perfect righteousness of Christ. That perfect righteousness is not invalidated by any sins of his. He is perfect in Christ; and until Christ is imperfect, the imperfections of the creature do not mar the justification of the believer in the sight of God.

If he falls into some glaring sin—O God, keep us from it!—if he falls into some glaring sin, he will go with broken bones, but he will reach heaven for all that. Although in order to try him and let him see his vileness, he is allowed to go far astray, yet He that bought him will not lose him; He that chose him will not cast him away; He will say unto him, *"I, even I, am he that blotteth out thy transgressions for mine own sake, and will not remember thy sins"* (Isaiah 43:25). David may go ever so far away, but David is not lost. He comes back and cries, *"Have mercy upon me, O God!"* (Psalm 51:1). And so shall it be with every believing soul— Christ will bring him back. Though he slip, he will be kept, and all the chosen seed shall meet around the throne.

If it were not for this last truth— though some may chafe at it—what would become of some of God's people? They would be given up to despair. If, dear reader, you are a backslider, I pray you make not a bad use of what I have said. Let me say to you, poor backslider, your Father yearns over you. He has not erased your name out of the registry. Come back, come back now to Him and say, "Receive me graciously, and love me freely." He will say, "I will put you among the children." He will pass by your backsliding and will heal your iniquities. You will yet stand once more in His favor and know yourself to be still accepted in the Redeemer's righteousness and saved by His blood.

God does not mean that His child will not be tried, or that he will not even sometimes fall under the trial. But He does mean this, once for all: *"He that believeth on Christ is not condemned."* At no time, by no means, is he under the sentence of condemnation, but is forevermore justified in the sight of God.

## Chapter 8

# What This Faith Includes

*There is therefore now no condemnation to them which are in Christ Jesus, who walk not after the flesh, but after the Spirit. For the law of the Spirit of life in Christ Jesus hath made me free from the law of sin and death.*
*—Romans 8:1-2*

If we are not condemned, then at no time does God ever look upon His children, when they believe in Christ, as being guilty. Are you surprised that I should put it so? I put it so again: from the moment when you believe in Christ, God ceases to look upon you as being guilty, because He never looks upon you apart from Christ. You often look upon yourself as guilty, and you fall upon your knees as you should do, weeping and lamenting. But even then, while you are weeping over inbred and actual sin, He is still saying out of heaven, "So far as your justification is concerned, you are all fair and lovely." You are as black as the tents of Kedar—that is yourself by nature. You are fair as the curtains of Solomon— that is yourself in Christ. You are black—that is yourself in Adam—but comely in the second Adam.

Oh, think of that! You are always in God's sight pleasing, always in God's sight lovely, always in God's sight as though you were perfect. For you are complete in Christ Jesus, and perfect in Christ Jesus, as the apostle puts it in Colossians 4:12. Always do you stand completely washed and fully clothed in Christ. Remember this. It is certainly included in the words, *"he that believeth on him is not condemned."*

Another great thought is this, you are never liable as a believer to receive punishment for your sins. You will be chastised on account of them, as a father chastises his child—that is a part of the Gospel dispensation—but you will not be smitten for your sins as the lawgiver smites the criminal. Your Father may often punish you as he punishes the wicked, but never for the same reason.

The ungodly stand on the ground of their own demerits. Their sufferings are awarded as their due deserts. But your sorrows do not come to you as a matter of desert—they come to you as a matter of love. God knows that in one sense your sorrows are such a privilege that you may count them as a blessing you do not deserve. I have often thought of that when I have been sorely troubled. I know some people say, "You deserved the trouble." Yes, my friends, but there is not enough merit in all the Christians put together to deserve such a good thing as the loving rebuke of our heavenly Father.

Perhaps you cannot see that. You cannot think that a trouble can come to you as a real blessing in the covenant. But I know that the rod of the covenant is as much the gift of grace as the blood of the covenant. It is not a matter of desert or merit. It is given to us because we need it. But question whether we were ever good enough to deserve it. We were never able to get up to so high a standard as to deserve so rich, so gracious, a providence as this covenant blessing—the rod of our chastening God. Never at any time in your life has a law-stroke fallen on you. Since you believed in Christ, you are out of the law's jurisdiction.

The law of England cannot touch a Frenchman while he lives under the protection of his own Emperor. *"For ye are not under the law, but under grace"* (Romans 6:14). The law of Sinai cannot touch you, for you are out of its jurisdiction. You are not in Sinai or in Arabia. You are not the son of Hagar or the son of a handmaid. You are the son of Sarah, have come to Jerusalem, and are free. You are out of Arabia and have come to God's own happy land. You are not under Hagar, but under Sarah, under God's covenant of grace. You are a child of promise, and you will have God's own inheritance. (See Galatians 4:22-31.)

Believe this, that never will a law-stroke fall on you. Never will God's anger in a judicial sense drop on you. He may give you a chastising stroke, not as the result of sin, but rather as the result of His own rich grace, which would get the sin out of you so that you may be perfected in sanctification, even as you are now perfect and complete before Him in the blood and righteousness of Jesus Christ.

## Chapter 9

# *What This Faith Excludes*

*For by grace are ye saved through faith; and that not of yourselves: it is the gift of God: Not of works, lest any man should boast.*
*—Ephesians 2:8-9*

**W**hat does faith exclude? Well, I am sure it excludes **boasting**. *"He that believeth is not condemned"* (John 3:18). Ah! if it said, "He that works is not condemned," then you and I might boast in unlimited quantity. But when it says, *"He that believeth,"* there is no room for us to say half a word for the old self.

No, Lord, if I am not condemned, it is Your free grace, for I have deserved to be condemned a thousand times since I sat down to write this. When I am on my knees and I am not condemned, I am sure it must be sovereign grace, for even when I am praying, I deserve to be condemned. Even when we are repenting, we are sinning, and adding to our sins while we are repenting of them.

Every act we do as the result of the flesh is to sin again, and our best performances are so stained with sin that it is hard to know whether they are good works or bad works. So far as they are our own, they are bad; and so far as they are the works of the Spirit, they are good. But, then, the goodness is not ours, it is the Spirit's, and only the evil remains to us. Ah, then, we cannot boast! Be gone, pride! Be gone!

The Christian must be a humble man. If he lifts up his head to say something, then he is nothing indeed. He does not know where he is or where he stands, when he once begins to boast, as though his own right hand had gotten him the victory. Quit boasting, Christian. Live humbly before your God, and never let a word of self-congratulation escape your lips. Sacrifice self, and let your song be before the throne, *"Not unto us, O LORD, not unto us, but unto thy name* [we] *give glory"* (Psalm 115:1).

What next does it exclude? I think it ought to exclude—now I am about to smite myself—it ought to exclude **doubts and fears**. *"He that believeth is not condemned."* How dare you and I draw such long faces and go about as we do sometimes as though we had a world of cares upon our backs? What I would have given ten or eleven years ago if I could have known that verse was assured to me, that I was not condemned! Why, I thought if I could feel I was once forgiven, and had to live on bread and water, and to be locked up in a dungeon, and every day be flogged with a cat-o'-nine-tails, I would gladly have accepted it, if I could have once felt my sins were forgiven.

Now, you are a forgiven man, and yet you are cast down! Oh, shame on you. No condemnation, and yet miserable? Fie, Christian! Get up and wipe the tears from your eyes. If there is a person lying in jail now, who is to be executed next week, and if you could go to him and say, "You are pardoned," would he not spring up with delight from his seat? Although he might have lost his goods, and though it would be possible for him after the pardon to have to suffer many things, yet, so long as life was spared, what would all this be to him? He would feel that it was less than nothing.

Now, Christian, you are pardoned, your sins are all forgiven. Christ has said to you, "[Your] *sins, which are many, are forgiven*" (Luke 7:47). Are you yet miserable? Well, if we must be so sometimes, let us make it as short as we can. If we must be sometimes cast down, let us ask the Lord to lift us up again. I am afraid some of us get into bad habits and have come to make it a matter of practice to be downcast.

Christian, mind it will grow upon you—that peevish spirit. If you do not resist that sinfulness at first, it will get worse with you. If you do not come to God to turn these doubts and fears out of you, they will soon swarm upon you like flies in Egypt. When you are able to kill the first great doubt, you will perhaps kill a hundred, for one great doubt will breed a thousand, and to kill the mother is to kill the whole brood.

Therefore, look with all your eyes against the first doubt, lest you should become confirmed in your despondency and grow into sad despair. *"He that believeth on him is not condemned."* If this excludes boasting, it ought to exclude doubts too.

Once more, faith excludes **sinning any more**. My Lord, have I sinned against You so many times, and yet have You freely forgiven me all? What stronger motive could I have for keeping me from sinning again? Ah, there are some who are saying this is licentious doctrine. A thousand devils rolled into one must the man be who can find any licentiousness here. What! Go and sin because I am forgiven? Go and live in iniquity because Jesus Christ took my guilt and suffered in my place instead? Human nature is bad enough, but I think this is the very worst state of human nature when it tries to draw an argument for sin from the free grace of God.

Bad as I am, I do feel this: it is hard to sin against a pardoning God. It is far harder to sin against the blood of Christ and against a sense of pardon, than it is to sin against the terrors of the law and the fears of hell itself. I know that when my soul is most alarmed by a dread of the wrath of God, I can sin with comfort compared with what I can tolerate when I have a sense of His love shed abroad in my heart.

What is more monstrous? To realize your title is clear, and yet sin? Oh, vile reprobate! You are on the borders of the deepest hell. But I am sure, if you are a child of God, you will say the same when you have discovered your title is clear, and feel yourself justified in Christ Jesus.

Now, for the love I bear his name,
What was my gain, I count my loss;
My former pride I call my shame,
And nail my glory to his cross.

Yes, I must and will *"count all things but loss for the excellency of the knowledge of Christ Jesus my Lord"* (Philippians 3:8). May my soul be found in Him, perfect in His righteousness! This will make you live near to Him. This will make you like Him.

Do not think that this doctrine, by dwelling on it, will make you think lightly of sin. It will make you think of it as a hard and stern executioner to put Christ to death, as an awful load that could never be lifted from you except by the eternal arm of God. Then you will come to hate it with all your soul, because it is rebellion against a loving and gracious God. You will, by this means, far better than by any Armenian doubts or any legal quibbles, be led to walk in the footsteps of your Lord Jesus, and to follow the Lamb whithersoever He goes.

I think this little work, though I have written it for the children of God, is meant for sinners, too. Sinner, I would desire that you did say so. If you know this, that *"he that believeth is not condemned,"* then, sinner, if you believe, you will not be condemned. May all that I have said help you to this belief in your soul.

Oh, but you say, "May I trust Christ?" As I said, it is not a question of whether you may or may not, you are commanded to do so. The Scripture commands the Gospel to be preached to every creature. The Gospel is, *"Believe in the Lord Jesus Christ and thou shalt be saved."* I know you will be too proud to do it, unless God by His grace should humble you. But if you feel that you are nothing and have nothing of your own, I think you will be very glad to take Christ to be your all-in-all. If you can say with poor Jack the Huckster:

"I'm a poor sinner and nothing at all,"

You may go on and say with him,

"But Jesus Christ is my all-in-all."

God grant that it may be so, for His name's sake. Amen.